PORTIS
LIFEBOATS

Nicholas Leach

ISBN 9781909540279

© Nicholas Leach 2022

- Published by Foxglove Publishing Ltd

- Foxglove House, Shute Hill, Lichfield, Staffs WS13 8DB

- m > 07940 905046, e > njl7@outlook.com

- Layout and design by Nicholas Leach/Foxglove Publishing

ACKNOWLEDGEMENTS

This book could not have been written without the help and support of personnel at Portishead lifeboat station, in particular Mike Roberts, Helen Lazenby and Ian Lazenby, who answered numerous queries and supplied many photographs, as well as being welcoming and supportive during my many visits to Portishead. The information about Pill lifeboat station from the files of the late Grahame Farr, eminent lifeboat historian and a native of Portishead, was also very useful. My thanks to the RNLI Heritage Team and Hayley Whiting for continuing to facilitate my research. Finally, my gratitude is extended to Ian Moignard for checking the finished work and, as usual, pointing me in the right direction with information and wording.

This is a non-official RNLI publication. Any views or opinions expressed in this publication are solely those of the author and do not necessarily represent those of the RNLI.

Contents

TIMELINE

1814 Act of Parliament governing the enclosure of land at Portishead for a public wharf was passed.

1824 National Institution for Preservation of Life from Shipwreck (NIPLS) founded in London.

1854 RNIPLS reformed and renamed Royal National Lifeboat Institution.

1860s A pier and deepwater dock was built by the Bristol & Portishead Pier and Railway for larger ships.

1867 The Portishead branch of the Great Western Railway (GWR) was opened on 12 April by the Bristol and Portishead Pier and Railway Company.

1880s Portishead Dock was acquired by Bristol Corporation, and was subsequently managed as part of the Port of Bristol until its closure.

1882 A lifeboat station was established at Weston-super-Mare by the RNLI.

1890 First steam-powered lifeboat, named Duke of Northumberland, enters service

1904 First RNLI motor lifeboat, a converted pulling and sailing lifeboat enters service.

1923 First twin-engined motor lifeboat enters service at New Brighton.

1926 Construction work started on Portishead A Power Station next to the dock, and it began generating electricity in 1929 for the Bristol Corporation's Electricity Department.

1933 A motor lifeboat was placed on station at Weston-super-Mare.

1940 On 30 May RNLI lifeboats were part of an armada of little ships involved in Operation Dynamo, the evacuation of the British Expeditionary Force from the beaches of Dunkirk.

1949 Construction of Portishead B Power Station began; it became operational in 1955.

1949 The power stations became a part of the nationalised electricity industry, and were operated in turn by the British Electricity Authority, the Central Electricity Authority and the Central Electricity Generating Board (CEGB).

1963 First inshore lifeboats enter service.

1966 An inshore lifeboat was supplied to Weston-super-Mare; a second ILB was sent in 1969.

1971 A lifeboat station at Pill was established, lasting for only four years before being closed in 1974.

1972 First Atlantic rigid-inflatable inshore lifeboat enters service.

1976 Portishead A Power Station closed; the first of its two chimney stacks was demolished in September 1981, followed by the second in August 1982.

1982 Portishead B Power Station closed.

1992 The Port of Bristol Authority finally closed the dock as industrial activities at the dock ceased with the closure of the power stations.

1995 Portishead Lifeboat Trust founded and a boathouse was built at Sugar Loaf Beach.

2008 The RNLI formally approved the adoption of Portishead Lifeboat Trust.

2015 Portishead lifeboat station established by the RNLI in a new lifeboat house at Eastcliff.

Portishead Lifeboats
INTRODUCTION

Portishead lifeboat station, its volunteers and supporters were adopted into the RNLI network in 2015. An impressive purpose-built lifeboat house to accommodate an Atlantic 85 and its launching rig was erected near Portishead Marina. The station is a vital link in the chain of rescue services covering the treacherous fast-flowing waters of the Bristol Channel. This book looks at the operations of the Portishead lifeboats and their crews under the auspices of the RNLI, and describes the previous life-saving services in the upper Bristol Channel, starting at Pill in the early 1970s and continued by the Portishead Lifeboat Trust.

▲ The entrance to Portishead Docks when ships and industry dominated the area. The site on which the RNLI station was built had originally been owned by the Crown, the Board of Trade, the City of Bristol and the Bristol & Portishead Pier and Railway Company and was made available to the railway company from 1870 to 1886. The original building served as a ticket office and waiting room. It was purchased by four gentlemen in Bristol in 1933 for £800 and served as a Masonic Lodge.

1971 – 1974
RNLI LIFEBOATS
AT PILL

Although the RNLI's involvement at Portishead formally began in 2015, an independent lifeboat was operated at Portishead before that, and in the 1970s the RNLI established an inshore lifeboat station at nearby Pill, which was operational for just three years from 1971 until 1974. The small town of Pill, on the south bank of the River Avon, was for

many generations connected with the Bristol pilots, the Westermen and hobblers, who tended vessels in the river and anchorages. The ferry crossing the Avon to Shirehampton is historic, dating from at least the mid-eighteenth century.

Moves to open the station began on the evening of 29 March 1971 when, in the Duke of Cornwall public house at Pill, Roderick (Dag)

Pike, Lifeboat Inspector for No.7 area, called a meeting to discuss with interested parties the opening of the station, the training of the crews, the area to be covered and the communications necessary for such operations, and to form a local committee.

Among those present were inspecting representatives from the Coastguard, representatives of the two police forces, the Port of Bristol Authority, the Parish Council, Urban District Council, Portishead Sailing Club, Pill Ferry Company (Pill-Shirehampton ferry), Pill Hobblers' Association and various other interested parties.

Mr Pike described the ILB which was to be provided: an 18ft McLachlan type, built of glass-reinforced plastic, with twin engines, similar to that stationed at Weston-super-Mare, the neighbouring station to the west. He spoke of the capabilities of the VHF radio, and local pilot John Rich gave some information on the VHF performance of the Port of Bristol pilot launches and the presence of certain blind spots in the upper Bristol Channel. The Port Authority representative also gave details of the watchkeeping arrangements at the signal stations at Walton Bay and Avonmouth South Pier.

The limits of operation were the Severn Bridge to the north and Clevedon to the west, from where coverage was provided by Weston-super-Mare lifeboat. Distress calls would be routed through the Coastguard who would alert the most suitable station to deal with the incident. Distress calls through the police or direct to the

▲ McLachlan ILB 18-02 making her debut at Pill on 8 July 1971. (Grahame Farr, by courtesy of the RNLI)

▲ 18-02 was painted blue with a light grey superstructure, while the heavily silt-laden river Avon meant that keeping her hull clean was a challenge. Although she was kept close to the slipways from which the Rowles family launched many of the most famous Bristol Channel sailing pilot cutters, the Pill lifeboats were never provided with a slipway.

honorary secretary would also be dealt with and, in some cases, such as 'man overboard' in the river, this would prove the speediest method. It was stressed that safety boats from the Clevedon and Portishead Sailing Clubs would still be required as part of the Inshore Rescue Scheme.

The Pill ILB was moored at the spare ferry mooring, which was accessible at any state of the tide. Pill was the traditional home of the Bristol Channel pilots and hobblers, and consequently there was a good pool of men from which to choose crews and reserve crews.

Over the course of the next three months preparations were made for the opening of the new station, and the ILB arrived at Pill on the morning tide of 8 July 1971. After the volunteer crews had undertaken several exercises, 18-02 (later numbered A-503) became

The first Pill lifeboat

The first ILB was the prototype McLachlan, numbered 18-02 and later A-503; she measured 18ft 6in overall, 16ft on the waterline, with a beam of 8ft and a depth overall of 7ft 3in. Originally fitted with a 90bhp Evinrude stern drive engine, she achieved a speed of 20.9 knots in calm water. The production McLachlans were built of glass-reinforced plastic, but the prototype was wooden-hulled.

◀ The arrival of McLachlan A-503 (formerly 18-02) at Pill on 4 May 1972 after her winter refit. She came by road from Littlehampton and was put into the water at the Port of Bristol Underfall Yard on Cumberland Road. (Grahame Farr, by courtesy of the RNLI)

▲ McLachlan ILBs 18-02 and glass reinforced plastic-hulled 18-004. The latter, later renumbered A-504, was stationed at Weston-super-Mare from 1970 to 1983.

▶ Lowering the twin outdrives on 18-02 at Bristol, where she had been brought by road, 4 May 1972. (Grahame Farr, by courtesy of the RNLI)

operational a few days later. The ILB was moored at the spare ferry mooring in the River Avon, at the mouth of Pill creek. John Rich, Bristol Channel pilot, was appointed honorary secretary. The terminal building of the Pill-Shirehampton ferry was made available for storing the gear and was used by the crew when they were assembling.

The first service was undertaken on 27 July 1971, when the lifeboat

Three photos of A-503 undertaking a demonstration for Pill Carnival Day, 20 May 1972, including a man overboard exercise. (Grahame Farr, by courtesy of the RNLI)

crew were tasked to search for a
body in the river. The next service
came four days later, when 18-02
brought four people to safety from
the yacht *Ark Royal*, which was
stranded on the Swash Bank, a
mudbank at the mouth of the Avon.
The yacht was crossing the bank on
a falling tide when she became stuck
and needed assistance.

Pill lifeboat was much in
demand during 1972, with 18-02,
having been renumbered A-503,
undertaking ten effective services.
On 7 June 1972 she launched to
help the sole occupant of an open
boat which had capsized off Black
Nore Point. Conditions in the
estuary were not as bad as expected,
and the lifeboat found the person
struggling ashore with several
people already in attendance and
assisting. Five days later A-503
stood by a barge which had broken

adrift from Sudbrook. On 2 July
1972 the ILB assisted in saving two
from the sailing dinghy *Bybrook*, and
two weeks later towed in the motor
yacht *Maria Jean*, landing her three
crew at the ferry slip. Two services
were performed in September and
on 3 October A-503 helped the
motor boat Rayon.

In June 1973 A-510, another
McLachlan, was sent to Pill. The
new boat had been completed by
William Osborne at Littlehampton,
and was one of the GRP-hulled
18ft 6in McLachlans. She performed
her first service on 24 June 1973,
going to help the cabin cruiser *Trail
Ranger*, which was adrift in Redcliff
Bay. On 22 July 1973 she towed
in the cabin cruiser *Edarna*, which
was adrift in the sole occupant of
Horseshoe Bend with engine trouble.

What proved to be the final year
of operation for Pill lifeboat, 1974,

◀ McLachlan A-510 making her first run after her arrival at Pill on 22 July 1973. She was built by William Osborne at Littlehampton and was fitted with a reinforcing shoe on her forefoot to combat wear when she came in contact with the ferry slip at Pill. After leaving Pill, she went to Ramsgate, where she served for nine years. (Grahame Farr, by courtesy of the RNLI)

▶ A-510 towing in the motor launch Cotteswool of Bristowe on Regatta Day, 20 July 1974. The launch had been drifting rapidly upriver on the tide after an engine failure. The final service by the Pill lifeboat took place on 19 August 1974, when A-510 went to the yacht Fiddler, which had capsized. The lifeboat crew helped to right the boat, and then towed her to moorings at St Pierre. (Grahame Farr, by courtesy of the RNLI)

was reasonably busy, with nine service launches, with A-510 helping dinghies, yachts and, on 23 June, craft taking part in a powerboat race. In total seven powerboats were assisted and towed to safety.

However, in 1974 questions about the viability of the station were being raised, as there were problems with the moorings in the Avon. Proposals for moving operations to Sugar Loaf Beach had been considered in January 1974, but nothing came of these, so operations continued for the year.

However, at the end of the 1974 season, A-510 was withdrawn and the station was closed. Several factors contributed to the withdrawal, including the opening of the Avon Bridge, which led to the closure of the ferry and consequent dispersal of crew members. In addition, the closure of Bristol City Docks to commercial traffic resulted in the river becoming silted up and shallower in the long term, and this inevitably reduced the amount of time per tide when the boat was operational.

Pill lifeboat service summary

1971	July 27	Body in the river, gave help
	Aug 1	Yacht Ark Royal, landed 4
	9	Small sailing boat, escorted
1972	June 12	Barge, stood by
	July 2	Sailing dinghy Bybrook, of Bristol, saved dinghy and assisted to rescue 2
	16	Motor yacht Maria Jean, saved yacht and 3
	Oct 3	Motor boat Rayon, gave help
	15	Yacht Anticone, saved yacht and 1
	22	Sailing dinghy Catastrophy, saved dinghy and 2
1973	July 22	Cabin cruiser Edarna, saved boat
	Aug 15	Open boat of Pill, gave help and landed 4
	Sep 22	Cabin cruiser Seawitch, saved boat and 2
1974	Apr 14	Cruising yacht Mandamar, saved yacht and 2
	June 23	Seven power boats and two dinghies, gave help
	July 25	Canal barge Scorpion, saved barge and 5
	28	Dinghy Flying Wild, saved dinghy and 3
	Aug 19	Yacht Fiddler adrift, saved yacht

Year	ILB	Launches	No service	Persons landed	Persons saved	Saved
1971	18-02	15	12	1	–	–
1972	A-503	10	4	–	4	8
1973	A-510	5	2	1	1	2
1974	A-510	9	4	–	3	10

▲ Barry Dock No.2 lifeboat Susan Ashley paying a visit to Pill on Regatta Day, 20 July 1974. The 41ft Watson motor class lifeboat was stationed at Sennen Cove from 1948 to 1972, and was moved to Barry in 1973 to supplement the then new 44ft Waveney 'fast' lifeboat, notably for use in shallower areas of the Bistol Channel. (Grahame Farr, by courtesy of the RNLI)

1995 – 2015

PORTISHEAD LIFEBOAT TRUST

▲ Ray Herbert was a key driving force in raising local support that enabled the Portishead Lifeboat Trust (PLT) to be created in 1995.

▶ The first lifeboat operated by the Portishead Lifeboat Trust was an unnamed Ribcraft boat, which served from 1996 to 12 June 2003. Pictured with the boat, left to right, are crew members Tony Daw, Taff Davies, and Adam Forrest.

Following the withdrawal of the lifeboat at Pill, incidents in the upper reaches of the Bristol Channel were covered by the RNLI's two inshore lifeboats at Weston-super-Mare, while the area off Portishead, for the next two decades or so, was covered by the Portishead Yacht and Sailing Club's rescue boat. However, in 1992 their rescue service was suspended, after twenty-five years of service, during which the boats undertook

228 launches, assisted 404 people and saved thirty-four lives. HM Coastguard was unable to fund it anymore and the local sailing club could not afford to continue with it.

During the early 1990s local people realised that, due to considerable activity in the area, a sea rescue service was definitely needed. They raised a petition within their community calling for the formation of such a service, which was presented to both

Woodspring and Portishead councils. They very kindly provided an initial £5,000 towards establishing the service, and local fundraising efforts provided the remainder.

A group of local people came forward to manage the service and, with the support of the local residents, the Portishead Lifeboat Trust (PLT) was established in September 1995. Its stated aim was 'to save and protect the lives of

▲ The Ribcraft Denbar Sage on exercise in March 2006, with Weston-super-Mare RNLI relief lifeboat Gordon England (B-701). (Nicholas Leach)

▶ The boathouse at Sugar Loaf Beach, pictured in April 2010, with the RIB Denbar Sage inside. (Nicholas Leach)

the general public in particular by provision of a lifeboat in the Severn Estuary centred at Portishead'. PLT was set up as a charitable company with the Charity Commission and Companies House with Don Remnant as Chairman, who served in the post until 1997. The other officers were Martyn Cruse (Treasurer), Colin Wilson (Secretary) and Ray Herbert (Trustee).

Within fifty-three weeks £30,000 had been raised, enough to have a lifeboat purpose-built for Portishead. The new 6.5m Ribcraft rigid-inflatable had been funded by local subscriptions and donations, and on 6 October 1996, just over a year after the Trust had achieved charity status, it was launched on its first service call from the boathouse. In its first financial year the Trust had a total income of £22,089.

The boathouse was constructed at Sugar Loaf Beach, adjacent to Portishead Yacht & Sailing Club. The site was almost two miles west of the docks, had a long slipway to the water, and was just down channel from Kilkenny Bay, about half way between Portishead Point and Black Nore Point. It offered a suitable

◀ The Ribcraft type rigid inflatable Denbar Sage on exercise off Portishead in March 2010. (Nicholas Leach)

▼ Denbar Sage on exercise off Portishead in March 2010. During her career, which ended in 2012, she launched 158 times and saved 11 lives. (Nicholas Leach)

▲ Barbara Palmer being presented with a framed photograph of Denbar Sage, the lifeboat she funded for the Portishead Lifeboat Trust. (Helen Lazenby/PLT)

a network of other supporters assisting in various aspects of running the service. A number of companies also helped, sponsoring equipment and providing kit, and Avon & Somerset Constabulary Training School and Kestrel Managed Workspaces both allowed use of their meeting rooms in Portishead for crew training.

The first boat served until June 2003, when it was replaced by a newer rigid-inflatable of the same type, which was named *Denbar Sage*. The boat was largely funded by Barbara Palmer, who donated £30,000 towards its cost. She formally named the boat at Sugar Loaf Beach with a bottle of Somerset cider, because, as Barbara explained, 'The lifeboat was built in Somerset, operates in Somerset, so had to be blessed using cider'.

Denbar Sage was in service from 2003 to 2012, during which time she assisted and saved many lives. On 28 August 2008, during a training exercise, the lifeboat was damaged by heavy seas. The crew sent out a 'mayday' which was answered by the RNLI lifeboat from Weston-super-Mare, the Severn Area Rescue Association (SARA) and a large Grimaldi car carrier heading out of port. The Portishead Lifeboat Trust borrowed a lifeboat from Geoff Dawe while repairs were undertaken to their own boat by Ribcraft.

Up to 8 May 2012 the Portishead Trust's lifeboats were called out on 321 operations, saved thirteen lives,

access to the challenging waters of the Bristol Channel, where the huge rise and fall of the tide often made launching and recovery extremely difficult, although the boathouse itself was somewhat cramped with only rudimentary crew facilities.

The Trust was headed by a Chairman, with a Board of Trustees responsible for operational and administrative matters and the allocation of funds. After Don Remnant, the subsequent Chairmen were Colin Wilson (1998-2009), John Gittings (2010-11), John McCorquodale (2011-14) and Mike Roberts (since 2014). The service was never short of enrolled crew and helms, with shore helpers and

▼ The name plate from Denbar Sage on display in the RNLI lifeboat house at Portishead. (Nicholas Leach)

The Atlantic 75 B-733, leased from the RNLI, being returned to the boathouse at Sugar Loaf Beach after a service. (Helen Lazenby/PLT)

The rather basic crew facilities inside the PLT boathouse at Sugar Loaf Beach. (Helen Lazenby/PLT)

and rendered assistance to another 400 persons, who might otherwise have got into serious difficulties.

Discussions between PLT and the RNLI took place over a number of years. In March 1995 the RNLI decided that there was insufficient evidence for them to establish a lifeboat station at Portishead, so the PLT continued independently. However, the relationship remained positive, with PLT sending crew members to the RNLI's College in Poole at various times for training, and adoption by the RNLI remaining on the PLT's agenda.

▶ Recovery of B-729 at Sugar Loaf Beach using the PLT's launching tractor in March 2012. B-729 served at Portishead from March 2011 to May 2013. She originally entered service with the RNLI in 1996 at Kilrush, on the west coast of Ireland.

Eventually, there was positive news and on 5 November 2008 the RNLI Trustees decided to approve the adoption of PLT, a decision confirmed by the RNLI Trustees at a meeting in April 2009. However, this was just the start of a fairly lengthy process as a new shore facility was needed for the RNLI to complete the adoption.

Between 2011 and 2015, while PLT was being adopted and a suitable location for a station was being found, the RNLI leased two Atlantic 75s to the PLT. The first was B-729, which served at Kilkeel for 14 years. She was replaced by the former Burnham-on-Crouch Atlantic 75 *Brandy Hole* (B-733), in May 2013, which remained until 2015.

▶ Swapping over lifeboats in the lock of Portishead Marina in March 2013, with B-733 arriving to take over from B-729. (By courtesy of Portishead RNLI)

An impressive line-up of Bristol Channel lifeboats, from Penarth, Weston-super-Mare and Burnham-on-Sea, as well as Portishead (second from right) during an exercise in February 2013. (Nicholas Leach)

◀ The Atlantic 75 B-729 (originally named Rose West and stationed at Kilrush) on exercise in the Bristol Channel, February 2013. She was leased to the Portishead Lifeboat Trust by the RNLI. (Nicholas Leach)

◀ The former Burnham-on-Crouch Atlantic 75 B-733, originally funded by Brandy Hole Yacht Club, served at Portishead for two years. She is pictured at the entrance to Portishead Marina in March 2015. (By courtesy of Portishead RNLI)

TIC 85 B-884 MY LADY ANNE

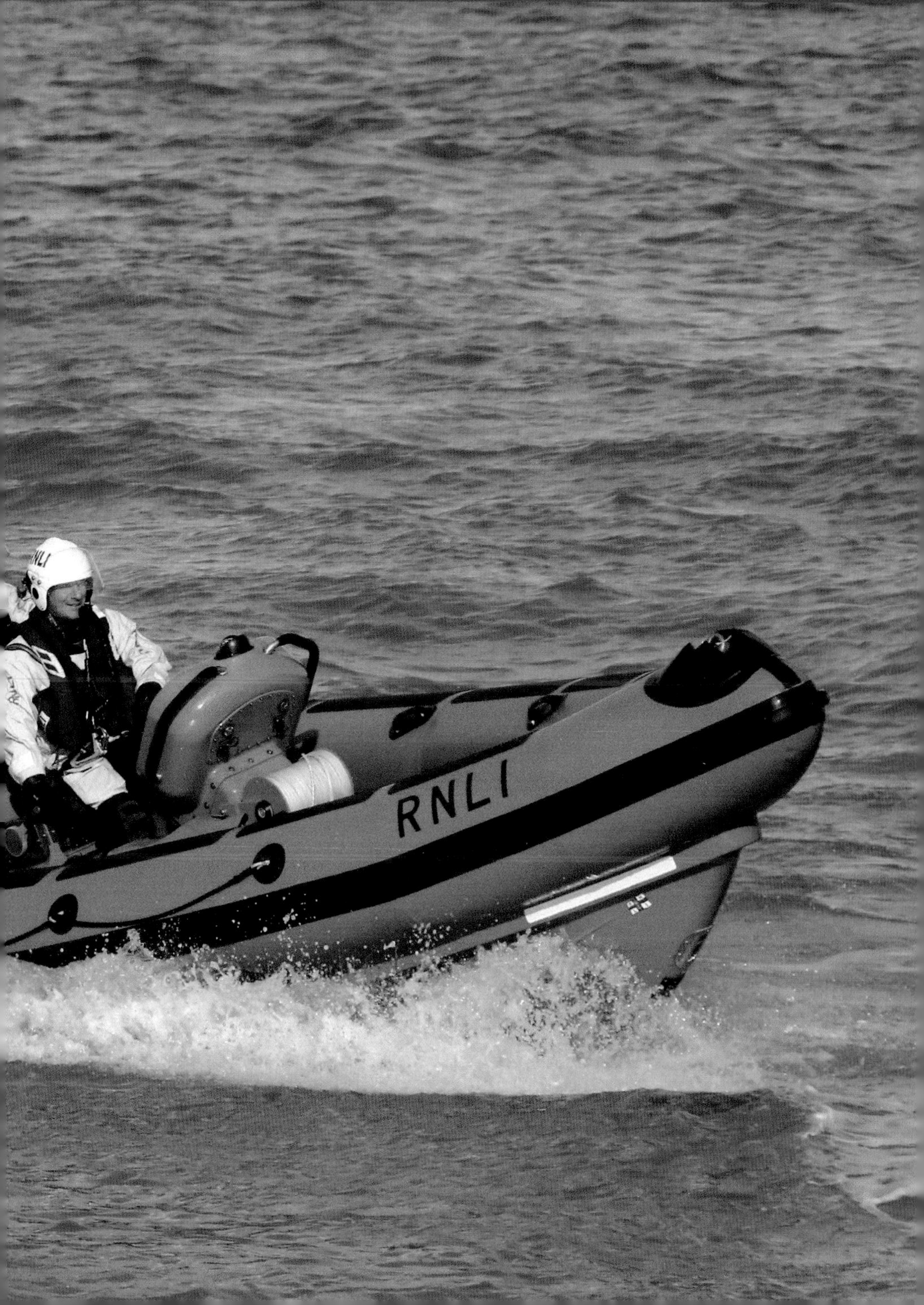

2015 –
THE RNLI ERA

Although Portishead lifeboat was well managed and maintained, adoption of the service by the RNLI was pursued, and in 2011 the RNLI's Trustees agreed to adopt the station, and bring its funding, maintenance and operations into the RNLI network. However, before the RNLI could further the matter a suitable site had to be acquired and the requisite shore facilities put in place to enable an Atlantic rigid inflatable ILB and its launching rig to operate effectively.

An extensive search of possible locations was undertaken, and eventually a site, occupied by the former Portishead Masonic Lodge, at the entrance to Portishead Marina, was selected. Work commenced on a new lifeboat station on 7 April 2014, with the demolition of the old Lodge, and the construction project lasted twelve months. After completing the build, battling all weathers and the area's difficult tidal conditions, contractors Andrew Scott handed the impressive new building into the care of the RNLI at the start of April 2015. The new lifeboat station included a large launching ramp, which cost almost £500,000 to construct, with its funding coming from a single specific donation.

When the project began, local fundraising was undertaken to provide £180,000 of the £1.9 million cost of the new building.

This was achieved in June 2014, much more quickly than expected, and so a new target to include funding of the crew room facilities, was set. Just a few months later, in December 2014, this extended target of £232,000 was also reached. The appeal was supported by the Portishead & Bristol Lifeboat Trust fundraisers and by RNLI branches in Somerset, Bristol, Gloucestershire, Bath and Worcester. The tireless efforts of these teams ensured that this was a real community effort.

Meanwhile, a Steering Group of senior PLT and RNLI personnel worked over a six-month period to plan the process of moving from a stand-alone independent organisation to being part of a large national organisation with well-developed processes and procedures. The Group covered many matters from managing

volunteers and their training, equipment and kit, to selecting officers, the use of boathouse equipment, the launching facilities and the arrangements for the arrival of a new lifeboat and tractor.

With the new station nearing completion, launching and recovery trials and training at the new site were undertaken using Clovelly's former Atlantic 75 *Spirit of Clovelly* (B-759),

▲ RNLI launch vehicles and Atlantic carriage being delivered to Portishead by landing craft, the only way to get the vehicles to the site, for trials to assess the best options for launching and recovery. (RNLI Portishead)

▲ Crew and fund-raisers at the old station at Sugar Loaf Beach say thank you to supporters and the community for helping to raise the money for the new station in June 2014. (Helen Lazenby)

▶ Work on the lifeboat house getting under way, July 2014. RNLI staff Adam Littlejohn (Coastal Engineering Manager) and David Jackman (Coastal Estates Engineer) were pivotal in planning the building. (Nicholas Leach)

▼ The new Portishead lifeboat station, designed and commissioned by the RNLI, pictured in April 2015 just before becoming operational. (Nicholas Leach)

which had been replaced by a new Atlantic 85 at the North Devon station in May 2014. She arrived at Portishead almost a year later and was involved in the crew training necessary to enable the station to become operational. It was gratifying for all those involved that the vast majority of volunteers, operational and non-operational, made the transition from the PLT to the new RNLI set-up.

On completion of Portishead's adoption, Mike Roberts (Chairman of PLT) was invited to become Chairman

of the Portishead RNLI Lifeboat Management Group and Bob Crane (PLT Launch Authority and Trustee) became the new Lifeboat Operations Manager (LOM), while Ian Lazenby became Senior Helm.

The adoption of the station by the RNLI was formalised at a ceremony on 24 April 2015, when the RNLI's flag was raised at the new lifeboat station, signalling that Portishead was part of the RNLI network, as *Spirit of Clovelly* (B-759) was declared operational. Volunteers and their families, as well as the founders and supporters of the PLT, gathered at the new lifeboat station for the event.

◀ Crew training using Atlantic 75 Spirit of Clovelly (B-759) on 19 April 2015, with the launching tractor TW41 and carriage at the ready. (Nicholas Leach)

◀ Launching and recovery training on 19 April 2015 with Atlantic 75 Spirit of Clovelly. The strong tidal currents of the Bristol Channel mean recovering the Atlantic stern first into the carriage can be a challenging operation. (Nicholas Leach)

▲ The Atlantic 75 B-759 Spirit of Clovelly being launched from the new lifeboat house after the formal raising of the RNLI flag on 24 April 2015. (Nicholas Leach)

▶ B-759 Spirit of Clovelly with the lifeboat house and the launching ramp, 24 April 2015. (Nicholas Leach)

▶ Recovery of B-759 Spirit of Clovelly after a short demonstration off the station, 24 April 2015. (Nicholas Leach)

Bob Crane, the first RNLI LOM, was invited by Nigel Jones, the RNLI's Divisional Operations Manager, to raise the RNLI flag at the new station. Nigel thanked the volunteers for all the hard work and commitment shown during the previous years to make the RNLI's adoption a reality, and presented a certificate of adoption, recognising Portishead as an operational asset of the RNLI, to Michael Roberts, Chairman of Portishead Lifeboat Management Group.

Meanwhile, on 9 May 2015 the last launch took place from the PLT's home of nearly twenty years, at Sugar Loaf Beach. Volunteer crew, supporters and founder members of the PLT mustered there to launch the Portishead & Bristol Lifeboat for the last time and bid farewell to the site.

Three of the Trust's longest serving volunteers, Tony Daw, Andy Allen and Adam Forrest, were selected to be the crew for the event, and admitted they were 'truly honoured' to be chosen. But as the Portishead & Bristol Lifeboat said goodbye to the base at Sugar Loaf Beach, and made her way around to the Marina, it became apparent that there was a yacht in trouble near the Marina entrance so the lifeboat was asked to assist, taking the yacht into the Marina as a final service.

New boathouse opened

With the lifeboat station up and running, the formal opening ceremony of the new boathouse took place on 20 June 2015. Over 300 guests were in attendance to celebrate the dawning of a new era

▲ Rev Philip Auden, the Deputy Lord Lieutenant of the City and County of Bristol and the station's padre. (Helen Lazenby)

▼ Ian Alder (volunteer lifeboat mechanic), Susan Beaton (crew) and Bruce DuPreez (helm) in April 2015. (Nicholas Leach)

▲ Bob Crane (on left) was the Launch Authority at PLT. He became the first LOM at the new RNLI station and had the honour of raising the RNLI flag for the first time, assisted by Nigel Jones, the RNLI's Divisional Operations Manager. (Nicholas Leach)

in Portishead lifeboat's history, recognising an anonymous donor who gave £500,000 to help fund the project in 2014.

The impressive new £1.9 million purpose-built lifeboat station was officially opened by Peggy Gittings, widow of the former PLT Chairman John Gittings, who sadly died earlier in the year before he was able to see the fruits of his efforts over many years. Mike Roberts, chairman of Portishead RNLI, addressed the crowd of supporters and well-wishers, saying it was a 'fantastic, exciting day', and added: 'Having this new building, which the RNLI has built, is great for all our volunteers. It actually has changing rooms and showers, and places to make tea, and things like that. We've been an independent lifeboat trust for the last nineteen years. In that time we've done over 380 rescue missions, but to be part of the RNLI is a big thing.'

The keys to the new station were formally handed over to Bob Crane by the RNLI Chairman, Charles Hunter-Pease, who also spoke about the impressive station, as Portishead was formally welcomed into the RNLI. At the end of the ceremony, *Spirit of Clovelly* (B-759) was launched for a short demonstration run, being joined by the privately-owned lifeboat *The Chieftain* (ex-ON.864), which was on hand to support the event.

A more low-key event took place on 20 August 2015, when the lifeboat crew, together with the Station Chaplain, Rev Philip Auden, held their own dedication ceremony for the lifeboat, which included a blessing of the boat with a bottle of traditional Somerset cider.

New Atlantic 85

The next step in the RNLI's takeover of the station was the provision of a new lifeboat, and on 14 September 2015 the new Atlantic 85 *My Lady*

◀◀ On 20 June 2015 the new lifeboat house was formally opened, with Vice Admiral Sir Tim Laurence handing over the building to the RNLI on behalf of the donors.

◀ Charles Hunter-Pease, RNLI Chairman, formally accepted the building on behalf of the RNLI.

◀ Peggy Gittings, with Emily Foster of the RNLI, formally opens the new lifeboat house.

◀◀ Bob Crane, the first LOM at the new RNLI station, speaks to the crowd at the boathouse opening ceremony.

▼ Atlantic 75 Spirit of Clovelly (B-759) is put through her paces at the end of the boathouse opening ceremony on 20 June 2015.

▲ Atlantic 75 Spirit of Clovelly (B-759) is put through her paces at the end of the boathouse opening ceremony on 20 June 2015, accompanied by the former Barmouth lifeboat The Chieftain, owned at the time by Tony Gatt. (Nicholas Leach)

▲ Front row (crouching): Paul Weston, Mark Burgoine, Ian Alder and Tony Daw, with (standing centre) Peggy Gittings, Charles Hunter-Pease; middle row (to left of Peggy Gittings): Jake Scott, Helen Lazenby, Jim Burtonwood, Susan Beaton and Andy Phillips, and (to right of Charles), Adam Forrest, Ian Reed, Tony Hancorn and Bob Crane; back row (to left of Charles' head): Chris Wade, Dave Hurst, Derek Weatherburn, Jake Bacon, Bernd Langheim, Steve Nelson, Richard Weston and Duncan Cook; back row (to right of Charles' head): Nick Williams, Jon Colwill, Neil Sutor and James Hart; on board lifeboat (left to right): Mike Chichester, Andy Weston and Ian Lazenby. (Nicholas Leach)

Anne (B-884) arrived from the RNLI's Inshore Lifeboat Centre at Cowes, where she had been built. She was the first Atlantic 85 to have been built entirely within the ILC. There followed an intensive period of crew familiarisation and training, with the lifeboat being launched and recovered numerous times as the crew got to know how to handle the boat and her equipment, and at 8pm on 17 September B-884 was declared operational. She undertook her first service on 19 September, being launched to search for two people reported to be in difficulty in the water.

On 5 March 2016 the new Atlantic 85 was formally named in front of hundreds of guests. The event was blessed with sunny skies and, despite a chilly northerly wind, everybody was in high spirits as the town's first new RNLI lifeboat was named and dedicated.

Vice-Admiral Sir Tim Laurence handed over the boat into the care of Portishead RNLI, and she was accepted by Bob Crane, who said: 'It is with great pride that we at Portishead accept this new Atlantic 85 class lifeboat. We have, together, come a long way since our start as Portishead Lifeboat Trust, with the move to our present location. The commitment and hard work from everyone has been of seriously epic proportions. Since we received this truly magnificent Atlantic 85 in September 2015, we have been called out on service fifteen times.'

The service of dedication was conducted by the Rev Philip Auden, after which the new Atlantic was christened My Lady Anne by Bill Wraith, of Tickhill, Doncaster, whose generous donation helped to fund the boat, in memory of his late wife. He said: 'This lifeboat is a fitting tribute to both my late

▲ Atlantic 75 Spirit of Clovelly (B-759) and Atlantic 85 My Lady Anne (B-884) together during the changeover from the former to the latter, 15 September 2015. (Nicholas Leach)

◄ Atlantic 75 Spirit of Clovelly (B-759) and Atlantic 85 My Lady Anne (B-884) in front of the newly-completed lifeboat house, 15 September 2015. (Nicholas Leach)

◄ Atlantic 75 Spirit of Clovelly (B-759) and Atlantic 85 My Lady Anne (B-884) in the waters of the Bristol Channel, 15 September 2015. (Nicholas Leach)

◀ Atlantic 85 My Lady Anne (B-884) being put through her paces on 15 September 2015 during crew training. (Nicholas Leach)

▼ My Lady Anne (B-884) being recovered up the ramp during initial crew training, 15 September 2015. (Nicholas Leach)

wife Anne and to the people who will crew her. I am proud to be associated with the RNLI and this lifeboat is a true demonstration that out of sadness, comes a wonderful lasting memory of Anne's life.' Bill had already funded one lifeboat, B-820, named Elizabeth Jane Palmer in memory of his daughter and stationed at Flamborough.

At the end of the ceremony, the lifeboat was launched for a short demonstration, joining an impressive parade of ex-lifeboats just off the boathouse. The four former RNLI lifeboats, all privately owned and based in and around the Bristol Channel and Portishead Marina, were: *The Always Ready* (ex-ON.766), owned by Craig Glassonbury; *Richard Vernon and Mary Garforth of Leeds* (ex-ON.931), owned by Bevis Musk; *Pentland* (ex-ON.940), owned by Dave Medri, volunteer shore crew at Portishead; and *Mary Irene Millar* (ex-ON.1151), helmed by Frank Smith MBE, former Coxswain of Salcombe lifeboat, and under the ownership of Keith Berry.

During 2016, the first full year of operations as an RNLI station,

Mike Roberts (above left) speaking during the naming and dedication ceremony of My Lady Anne (B-884) on 5 March 2016. The boat was named (left/right) by Bill Wraith in memory of his late wife, with (above right, left to right) Chris Wade, Jon Colwill, Paul Weston and Andy Phillips, and many others, in attendance.

The scene during the naming and dedication ceremony of My Lady Anne on 5 March 2016, with crowds at the boathouse (above), and able to watch the new lifeboat (above left and left) being launched and put through her paces, accompanied by four historic lifeboats. They were (main photo, left to right) Mary Irene Millar (ex-ON.1151), Richard Vernon and Mary Garforth of Leeds (ex-ON.931), Pentland (ex-ON.940) and The Always Ready (ex-ON.766).

▲ John and Peggy Gittings were involved in the PLT. Peggy opened the new lifeboat house and supports fundraising events. (RNLI Portishead)

▲ Ian Lazenby, pictured on board the Atlantic 85, became the station's Senior Helm when the RNLI adopted the station in 2015. (Nicholas Leach)

▲ Jake Scott retired as Helm and crew on 14 August 2020, after twenty-two years of voluntary service at Portishead (Helen Lazenby)

the volunteers, many of whom had served with the PLT, had their busiest year, launching fifty-one times on service. Among the many incidents during the year was one on 9 October. At 3.01pm, as the crew had returned from a training session, they were paged by Milford Haven Coastguard, who had picked up a faint 'mayday Portishead' call. Working with the Coastguard helicopter and Coastguard shore teams from Portishead and Chepstow, the lifeboat undertook an extensive search of the Bristol Channel from Clevedon up to and beyond the Severn Crossing. After two hours, the rescue teams were stood down as nothing was found.

Two call-outs towards the end of 2016 saw the total number of launches for the year top fifty. During the evening of 15 December 2016 the lifeboat was launched to a yacht which had come adrift from its mooring on the River Avon near to Marine Parade, Pill. The owner was trying to tow it back to its mooring by rowing in his tender with a line attached, but this was proving difficult despite the calm conditions, so the lifeboat took him back to Portishead Cruising Club. Two days later the volunteers undertook their fifty-first call out of the year, which coincidentally came as helm Jon Colwill was celebrating his fifty-first birthday. He left the celebrations to take his place as the crew went to help a kayaker in Clevedon. The lifeboat crew located him, and found him safe and well and not in need assistance.

On 1 May 2017 Bob Crane retired as the station's Lifeboat Operations Manager, having been a volunteer in Portishead for almost twenty years. Bob was asked by the Chairman to join the Portishead Lifeboat Trust in 1998, and become their Deputy Launch Authority. With all his experience and passion to help keep people safe on the water, he became the Launch Authority and went on to perform a similar role when the RNLI took over.

During the evening of 23 June 2017 the Atlantic 85 was launched to a yacht with five people on board, who were about to be stranded as the yacht had gone aground at high water, and the receding spring tide meant that their vessel could be stuck for hours. The lifeboat reached the casualty within a few minutes, and the crew threw lines to the yacht, pulling it to deeper water with just half a metre of water under the Atlantic's hull.

However, large waves made setting up a tow line challenging, and as the yacht's skipper tried to get his craft away from the mud using the engine, a rope became tangled around the propeller. After a check to make sure the casualties were well, the yacht was towed to Portishead Marina. Ian Lazenby, the helm, said afterwards: 'The crew of the casualty vessel were well equipped; it was just unfortunate that they were caught out. If the skipper had left it much longer to call us, it could have been a different story. We had to work fast to help, but my experienced crew were quick thinking and worked very well together to bring the yacht to safety.'

On a number of occasions Portishead lifeboat has worked with lifeboats from neighbouring stations, and one such incident came shortly after 7.25pm on 1 June 2019. A number of lifeboats and rescue services were alerted to an incident in the Bristol Channel, with both Penarth's inshore lifeboats being tasked, as was My Lady Anne from Portishead. The

▼ The impressive lifeboat house at Portishead, home to the Atlantic 85, launching vehicle and crew training and changing facilities. (Nicholas Leach)

▲ HM Coastguard helicopter 187 landed on the foreshore at Portishead on 8 August 2020 after the helicopter and Portishead lifeboat volunteers went to help a person on a small rigid inflatable boat just off Denny Island, Portishead, who had suffered a suspected broken leg. Chris Wade, helmsman, said: 'It was a particularly challenging shout due to the rapidly ebbing tide and the number of boats with anchor lines very close by [the casualty]. The fractured leg was also complicated so we worked as fast as we could to recover the casualty on to our boat before we ran aground. Then liaising with Helicopter 187, we agreed how best to get the casualty to hospital. It was decided our best course of action was to recover to our slipway and then transfer the casualty to the helicopter. It was a difficult job in oppressively hot conditions, but everyone worked incredibly well to bring about a good outcome. I am very proud to be part of such a great team.' (Helen Lazenby/RNLI Portishead)

lifeboats were quickly on scene, and, together with SARA independent lifeboats, Coastguard rescue teams from Clevedon and Chepstow and Rescue Helicopter 187 from St Athan, they carried out a thorough search but, as nothing was found, the lifeboats were stood down and returned to their stations.

During 2020 operations at the station were affected by the Covid-19 pandemic and the lockdown, which restricted training for about six months and meant

▶ Atlantic 85 My Lady Anne (B-884) towing a yacht back to the marina. (Nicholas Leach)

that plans to mark the station's fifth anniversary as part of the RNLI network had to be postponed. But the lifeboat remained on call throughout the lockdown, and answered many calls.

Prior to the pandemic taking hold, on 1 March 2020 the lifeboat crew had a busy day. The Atlantic was launched on a training exercise, with the volunteer crew having been asked to scatter the ashes of a crew member's father-in-law, the family wishing to see him laid to rest in the Bristol Channel. The four crew members launched the lifeboat in a sombre mood and headed into position ready for the family and Lifeboat Padre to take part in the ceremony. A call then came in to say there was someone in trouble, so the lifeboat immediately headed to the casualty, finding a person in difficulty in a small vessel off Battery

Point, struggling to get back to shore. With the casualty close to the busy shipping lane, it was essential that they were located quickly and, within two minutes of being tasked, the lifeboat was on scene. The crew checked the casualty and took them to the lifeboat station. This speedy rescue took just five minutes to execute, from being tasked to recovering the casualty.

▲ Atlantic 85 My Lady Anne (B-884) on exercise off Portishead. (Nicholas Leach)

▼ Recovery of My Lady Anne on her purpose-built carriage, with Talus MB764 tractor TW41. (Nicholas Leach)

VOLUNTEER CREW AND STATION OFFICIALS 2022

ANDY CLARKE
Crew

ANDY PHILLIPS
Crew and Helm

ANDY WESTON
Crew and Helm

BRUCE DU PREEZ
Crew and Helm

CHRIS WADE
Crew and Helm

DAVE HODGES
Crew, Helm, Lifeboat Training Assessor

EMMA TILKE
Crew

GARETH LLOYD
Crew and Deputy Station Mechanic

IAN ALDER
Crew, Helm and Station Mechanic

IAN LAZENBY
Crew and Helm

IAN REED
Crew

JAKE BACON
Crew and Helm

JEM SMALE
Crew

JON COLWILL
Trainer and Shore Crew

LU SHEPHARD
Crew

MARC WARD-JENKINS
Crew

MIKE CHICHESTER
Crew, Helm, Lifeboat Training Assessor

NEIL SUTOR
Crew, Helm and DLA

NICK WILLIAMS
Crew

OLIVER COFFMAN
Crew

PAUL WESTON
Crew and Helm

SIMON LYNN
Crew, Lifeboat Training Coordinator

SUSAN BEATON
Crew

DAVE SLACK
Lifeboat Operations Manager

TONY HANCORN
Deputy Launching Authority

ADAM FORREST
Boathouse Manager and Shore Crew

SIMON PERKS
Fundraising Coordinator

MIKE ROBERTS
Station President

GEOFF VIAN
Hon Treasurer and Education Organiser

RICHARD THOMSON
Lifeboat Medical Officer

SIMON CHAPMAN
Station Chairman and Padre

LESLEY HIBBERD
Lifeboat Admin Officer

SADIE TAYNTON
Lifeboat Admin Officer

HELEN LAZENBY
Lifeboat Press Officer

SCOTT EGGINS
Deputy Lifeboat Press Officer

DAVE HURST
Shore crew, Deputy Station Mechanic

CAMERON JOHN
Trainee crew

MATT WALKER
Trainee crew

SAM BUTTS
Trainee crew

GRAHAM TULLETT
Trainee crew

TOM HAMPSON
Trainee crew

ANDY ALLEN
Shore crew

ANDY GAY
Shore crew and DLA

EMMA BERGER
Shore crew

LAURA PALMER
Shore crew

MATT LAZENBY
Shore crew

NATALIA WESTON
Shore crew

NOELLE FINCH
Shore crew

PHIL SMITH
Shore crew

PHIL SELWOOD
Shore crew

LIFEBOATS AND RESCUES

Years on station	ON	Name (if any) / Donor	Type / Notes
Oct 1996 – Jun 2003	–	*Portishead lifeboat* Local subscription and donations.	6.5m Ribcraft RIB
Jun 2003 – Mar 2011	–	*Denbar Sage* Gift from Barbara Palmer; the name comes from Dennis and Barbara, brother and sister; Sage was the family name.	6.5m Ribcraft RIB
Mar 2011– May 2013	B-729	*Rose West* Bequest of Miss Rosemary Dora Bodenham West.	Atlantic 75 Originally Kilrush
May 2013– Apr 2015	B-733	*Brandy Hole* Fundraising activities by Brandy Hole Yacht Club.	Atlantic 75 Originally Burnham
Apr 2015– Sep 2015	B-759	*Spirit of Clovelly* Clovelly Lifeboat Trust.	Atlantic 75 Originally Clovelly
Sep 2015–	B-884	*My Lady Anne* Gift of Bill Wraith in memory of his late wife.	Atlantic 85

Year	Total calls	Total people assisted	Total dogs assisted	Lives saved
2015	25	25	1	0
2016	52	60	4	2
2017	41	33	0	0
2018	37	30	1	0
2019	36	31	5	3
2020	39	26	0	1
2021	41	39	1	1